Should I be a Vegetarian?

A personal reflection on meat-eating, vegetarianism and veganism

Neil Paul Cummins

Cranmore Publications

A catalogue record for this book is available from the British Library

ISBN: 978-1-907962-12-7

Published by Cranmore Publications

Reading, England

For Andrea

I eat therefore I am

... and I am what I eat

Contents

Preface

About 20 years ago I started calling myself a vegetarian. At this time I stopped eating all meat from animals with the exception of fish. When I tell someone that I am a vegetarian I, as most vegetarians surely do, usually get asked why I decided to become a vegetarian. Recently I realised that calling myself a vegetarian upsets some people (because I eat fish) so I now usually call myself a 'pescetarian'.

When asked why I decided to become a pescetarian I have not usually been able to come up with a cogent reply. At the time it just felt like the right thing to do.

Recently I have been reflecting more on my decision to become a pescetarian and the reasons why I should perhaps become a 'full-blown' vegetarian or vegan. Why did I feel like I should stop eating non-fish animals but continue to eat fish? Are there good reasons behind this feeling/decision?

In this book I explore a range of reasons why I, and you, might want to be a vegetarian, a pescetarian or a vegan.

Introduction

Why should one become a vegetarian? If you were to ask a group of vegetarians why they decided to become vegetarian you will, in all likelihood, get a diverse range of answers. Four of the most probable answers are the following:

1 It is not right to eat other animals. They are our companions and should be treated as such.

2 Eating meat is bad for the health of the human who eats it.

3   Treating animals as food-sources results in a 'violent attitude' which ultimately leads to increased violence in human society.

4   Eating animals is acceptable. The problem is that in modern industrialised societies we treat animals as resources which should be utilised to maximise profitability. It is this mentality which leads to unacceptable suffering and/or deleterious health effects in the humans who eat meat and/or increased violence in human society. If animals were viewed as individuals and treated with

respect then eating them would not result in such deleterious effects.

In the first four chapters of the book I consider each of these four positions in turn. Then, in *Chapter Five,* I draw some conclusions.

Chapter 1

It is not right to eat other animals

Some people decide to become a vegetarian, a pescetarian or a vegan for the sole reason that they believe that all animals are intrinsically valuable in themselves. These people believe that all animals are individual life-forms with their own desires and, in particular, they believe that all animals have their own desire to stay alive. On the extreme version of this view it would be as unacceptable to eat any animal as it would be to eat another human.

On this extreme view all animals are precious, all animals are our companions, and all animals should be treated with the respect and dignity that is shown to other humans. Or, to put this another way, one should not treat a non-human animal with less respect than one would treat a human.

There are, of course, less extreme versions of this view. One can believe that there are important differences between animals and that these differences mean that some animals are intrinsically valuable in themselves whereas other animals are not intrinsically valuable in themselves. If such a division is envisioned as existing between animals then one would have a good reason to believe that it is acceptable to eat some animals but unacceptable to eat other animals.

What differences between animals could create such a division? At a broad level one could believe that some non-human animals are sufficiently 'human-like' that they deserve to be treated like humans. So, some people ask the question: Are there non-human persons? Of course, this raises the question of what, exactly, a human 'person' is! Perhaps the concept of a 'person' is used to refer to animals which have knowledge of their own existence. If this is right, then any animal which has such knowledge is a person.

If such a division in the animal kingdom is envisioned to exist between animals which are sufficiently 'human-like' (or animals which are persons) and animals which are not sufficiently human-like (non-people?) then there would be a good reason to believe that it is acceptable to eat some animals, whilst it is not acceptable to eat other animals.

You will have noticed that I have been referring to 'envisioned' differences between animals rather than to 'actual' differences between animals. This is because it is very difficult (if not impossible) to tell what it is like to exist as a particular non-human animal. What happens is that humans observe the appearance and behaviour of non-human animals and form a judgement as to how 'human-like' these animals appear to be. So, chimpanzees, bonobos, dolphins and dogs might appear to humans to be sufficiently 'human-like' to be intrinsically valuable in their own right and should not, therefore, be eaten by humans. However, fish, sheep and cows might appear to be sufficiently 'un-human like' that one decides that these animals are not intrinsically valuable and, therefore, that it is acceptable to eat these animals.

In short, one's decision as to which animals are sufficiently 'human-like' to be intrinsically valuable in their own-right is not based on actual differences between animals; rather, such a decision is based on one's beliefs. Of course, it is very unlikely that one's beliefs are going to match a division that actually exists within the animals that exist on the Earth. One might believe that a dog is sufficiently 'human-like' but that a sheep is not sufficiently 'human-like'. But whether there is actually a real division in the world – an important attribute that a dog possesses but that a sheep does not possess – is a different matter entirely.

Now that I have outlined how one can envision there to be divisions within the animals on the Earth one can see one reason why one might decide to be a pescetarian. One might envision fish to be sufficiently 'un-human like' that one thinks it is acceptable to eat fish, whilst one could envision sheep, cows and birds to be sufficiently 'human-like' that one has no desire to eat such animals. Of course, one could envision such a distinction and also believe that there are many other animals which are sufficiently 'un-human like' that it is acceptable to eat them – animals such as rats, frogs and snails.

So, one can believe that it is not right to eat any animals, or one can believe that it is acceptable to eat some animals but not to eat other animals.

It is, perhaps, worth considering the following scenario. Let us imagine a vegetarian (which, let us remind ourselves, means a non-fish-eater) who believes that it is not right to eat fish because fish are intrinsically valuable and should be able to pursue their own desire to live without being killed by humans. Let us further imagine that this vegetarian comes across a fish that has died of 'natural' causes (old age!). Might this vegetarian consider it acceptable to eat the fish? Such an act of eating would seemingly not contravene the value system of the individual so they might well decide that it is acceptable for them to eat the fish. Such an eating would, seemingly, be more likely if the human was very hungry and stranded somewhere without alternative food sources.

Of course, a similar scenario could be constructed with non-fish animals such as a sheep which has died of natural causes. In short, one might find the idea of eating any animal to be acceptable if that animal has died of natural causes, but also be firmly opposed to the idea of killing an animal or interfering with the natural way of life of a living animal.

What of our vegan? Our vegan might place such a high intrinsic value on the existence of all animals that they believe that it is not right for humans to use any animal products (there are, of course, other possible reasons for becoming a vegan). Whilst, there are surely vegetarians who believe that it is acceptable to use some animal products such as honey but that it is not acceptable for humans to use animal products such as eggs.

What should be clear from the foregoing discussion is that there are lots of factors in play in the decision making process as to whether or not one should be a pescetarian, a vegetarian or a vegan. One might envision there to be important differences between living animals, and one might also envision there to be important differences between animals which are living and those which have died of 'natural' causes. The situation one is presently in may also be an important factor in one's decision making. If one is surrounded by a plentiful supply of non-animal food then one might be a vegan. However, if one finds oneself in a place, such as the Arctic, where eating fish seems to be necessary for one's survival then one might decide that it is acceptable to be a pescetarian.

Let us now complicate the situation much further by considering other factors that might come into play in one's decision making as to whether or not to be a vegetarian, a pescetarian or a vegan – factors relating to one's own health.

Chapter 2

Eating meat is bad for one's health

Some people decide to become a vegetarian, a vegan or a pescetarian, simply because they are concerned with their own health. These people might consider humans to be the only intrinsically valuable animals on the Earth, or they might not even have considered the issue of the intrinsic value of animals.

This belief might have been in play at some level when I myself became a pescetarian. When the feeling came over me to stop eating non-fish meat it was around the time that the BSE outbreak occurred in the UK. Surely eating beef at such a time might not have been conducive to one's good health.

One extreme view is simply that eating meat is bad for human health irrespective of any other factors. One might believe this because one believes that the human digestive system evolved to fit a non-meat-eating lifestyle. If one believes such a thing then one might believe that a lot of the diseases which exist in modern society are associated with humans eating products which are not wholly compatible with the human body (meat being one such product).

Of course, one could believe that certain types of meat are compatible with the human digestive system but that others are not. If so, then one might have a good reason to be a pescetarian – one might believe that eating fish is good for one's health, but that eating non-fish meat is bad for one's health.

A less extreme view is that the human health impacts of eating meat are closely intertwined with the life of the animal that is eaten. There are many potentially important factors at play in the life of the animal that is eaten. Let us consider two extremes. At one extreme is an animal that has lived a long and happy life in comparative freedom, able to live in a natural environment and fulfil its desires to the best of its ability which then dies in a natural way. One could envision that eating such an animal would not be harmful to one's health.

At the other extreme let us consider an animal that has lived its entire life in unnatural conditions, living in a small space which has been enclosed by humans to keep lots of these animals contained together in one place. These animals are not free to pursue their natural desires and live a life of comparative suffering and misery. Such animals might also be injected with chemicals or fed artificial foods in order to boost their productivity. One could easily envision that eating such an animal would not be conducive to one's good health.

These are the two extremes. There seem to be two important factors in play within these extremes. Firstly, is the animal itself being fed foods (or injected with things) which are not conducive to its own health? If so, eating such an animal might have deleterious impacts for the health of the human that eats this animal. Secondly, is the animal itself leading a happy life? If not then it is possible that the suffering and misery that this animal experiences in its life are somehow transferred into the human that eats the animal. There is already some evidence that when organs are transplanted from one human to another human that the memories of the donor are also transported, so it is respectable to believe that the memories of suffering of an animal can be transported into the body of the human who eats the flesh of this animal.

So, there are three reasons why one might believe that eating animals could have deleterious health impacts. Firstly, one could believe that eating meat is simply not fully compatible with the structure of the human body/digestive system. Secondly, one could believe that when animals are treated as resources and fed/injected with 'un-natural' products that it is bad for one's health to eat such animals. Thirdly, one could believe that the suffering experienced by animals is transported into one's body when one eats an animal which has suffered.

Clearly, if one believes either or both of the second and third reasons above then one is likely to either be a vegetarian/pescetarian/vegan or to be very careful about which types of meat one eats; alternatively, one might have a good reason to reduce one's meat consumption. It is also likely that one would have a preference for animals which have lived a relatively natural existence (such as fish, or free-range eggs, or organic and sympathetically reared animals) rather than animals which have been factory-farmed.

One can see that anyone who believes in one, or both, of the second and third reasons is also likely to have a good reason to be a pescetarian. This is because fish typically live a natural life free of human enclosure and/or artificial feeding/injections. However, it seems likely that fish do suffer at the moment they are killed, and the extent of this suffering and how it might become embedded in the body of the fish is hard to ascertain. What does seem likely is that the momentary suffering at the moment of death is likely to be less than the suffering embedded in a body from a life-long existence pervaded by suffering. And, of course, it should be remembered that fish-farming where fish are enclosed by humans and fed by humans is now occurring and increasing in scale.

If one believes any of the three reasons above (when modified from the meat of animals to animal products) then one is also likely to have a good reason to want to be a vegan. So, one might believe that eating dairy products is not fully compatible with the human body/digestive system. Or, one could decide that given that many dairy cattle are treated as resources, that it is safer to not consume any dairy produce. Or, one could believe that the suffering that is embedded in the meat of the body of an animal also becomes embedded in animal products associated with that body. If one believes any of these things one would have a good reason either to reduce one's consumption of animal products or to become a vegan.

So, one can see that there are good reasons either for becoming a vegan, or to be very careful about which animals one eats. It is possibly better to eat animals that have had a relatively natural and happy life.

There are no conclusive answers to these worries – particularly those relating to the memory transfer of suffering into the body of the eater. However, we can see that when one is deciding whether or not one should be a vegetarian/pescetarian/vegan that there are a great number of factors in play concerning human health, in addition to all of those factors relating to the intrinsic value of animals which we considered in the previous chapter. Let us now consider another group of factors – those relating to how the treatment of animals as a food source might lead to increased violence in human society.

Chapter 3

Increased violence in human society

In the previous two chapters I have considered two types of reasons why some people decide to become a vegetarian, a vegan, or a pescetarian – they believe that animals are intrinsically valuable and/or they are concerned with their own health. Some people decide to become a vegetarian/pescetarian/vegan for a very different reason, they believe that envisioning and treating animals as food-sources involves a 'violent attitude' which ultimately leads to increased violence in human society.

So, one can believe that no animals except humans have any intrinsic worth, that there are no deleterious health impacts for the individual human who eats animals or animal products, and still decide that it is a good idea to become a vegetarian or a vegan. If one believes that the envisioning and treating of animals as food resources leads to increased violence in human society then it is likely that one will aspire to see a world in which every human on the planet is a vegan.

There are many ways in which the eating of meat could lead to increased violence in human society. One of the most obvious possibilities is simply that acts of violence breed other acts of violence. In other words, one can believe that if one mistreats animals it is more likely that one will, as a consequence, also mistreat fellow humans; that is to say, when humans kill non-human animals it is more likely that humans will also be violent towards fellow humans. This consequence can be envisioned to occur both within the life of an individual human or to spread from one human to another human. In other words, if an individual human kills (or is violent towards) an animal one could believe that it is more likely that this particular human will be violent towards a fellow human. Alternatively, one could believe that the mere fact that we live in a society where there are factories in which groups of humans kill groups of animals, and that this is well-known – on the television/in newspapers/talked about – means that it is more likely that a human who has not killed an animal will be violent towards a fellow human.

This scenario does seem to be very plausible. You can probably find similar analogies from your own life. Habits and ways of living can be infectious/ become embedded. For me, I am more likely to eat healthy foods if I am with other people who are eating healthy foods. And once one starts eating slightly more healthily it is more likely that this will become sustained in the future. Whilst, if one repeatedly encounters television programmes or newspaper articles concerning the benefits of healthy eating (or has friends who start eating more healthily) then it is more likely that one will make the change oneself.

Irrespective of whether things are 'positive' or 'negative' small changes or individual actions have a tendency to spread out and lead to future consequences which might be hard to foresee at the time of the initial action. So, one of the consequences of the killing of animals by *some* humans might be that *other* humans are violent towards each other. Violence has, in a sense, become embedded in the fabric of society through the existence of factory farms and slaughter houses.

I have discussed the mass killing of animals in slaughter houses. Is the situation any different when individual animals are hunted and killed in the wild?

On the one hand, this does seem to be different because it is more 'natural' rather than a 'mechanised product line of killing'. On the other hand, there doesn't seem to be any getting away from the fact that acts of violence/killing seem to inevitably beget (or increase the likelihood of) further acts of violence/killing. So, perhaps the effects of such 'natural' killing are still deleterious but less pronounced – less harmful – than the effects of 'mechanised' killing.

So, there are good reasons why one might want to become a vegetarian/pescetarian/vegan. One can believe that the more animals that are killed by humans the more this way of being will become embedded in human society and the longer it will exist in the future, and that such killing leads to present and future violence between humans. By becoming a vegetarian/pescetarian/vegan one can initiate a small change which will hopefully have positive impacts in both the present and the future.

If one believes that it is factory farms and slaughter houses that are the primary centers of suffering and violence then one might have reason to believe that eating a fish which has been line-caught from the ocean is acceptable. One might believe this because one believes that compared to the former activities such an action entails relatively little violence and suffering. So, one might find it acceptable to be a pescetarian rather than a vegetarian/vegan.

It should be stressed that one can be a pescetarian rather than a vegetarian and still not eat any dairy products or other animal products. Contrarily, a vegetarian could eat lots of animal products. If one is a pescetarian who only eats a single animal related thing (meat or animal product) – fish – then one could be in some sense more 'animal friendly' than many vegetarians. On the subject of this chapter – the pescetarian lifestyle could possibly initiate less human violence in the future than a vegetarian lifestyle. But this would vary from case to case, and the ideal situation is clearly to be a vegan.

There is a more radical belief that one could have relating to the link between treating animals as resources and suffering/violence in human society. If one believes (possibly inspired by quantum entanglement) that the universe is deeply intercon- nected then one could envision factory farms and slaughter houses as 'centers of suffering/violence' which radiate out to other parts of the planet. So, these 'centers' could be locations which give rise to things such as a plethora of acts of violence and thoughts of violence (as whole animals get chopped into small pieces by humans with big knives). They could also be locations in which suffering is at a very heightened level (due to the experiences of the animals). If one believes that the universe is deeply interconnected then one could believe that such centers of suffering/violence radiate out feelings of suffering/violence to other parts of the Earth and that they thereby increase the likelihood of violent acts occurring between humans. Contrarily, centers of peace/happiness would radiate out more desirable impacts into their surroundings.

Having considered a third group of reasons why one might want to become a vegetarian, a pescetarian or a vegan, let us now consider the view that eating animals in itself is acceptable.

Chapter 4

Eating animals is acceptable...but

Let us now consider the view that is, in effect, the opposite view to the one we considered in *Chapter One*. This is the view that it is *in principle* acceptable for humans to eat non-human animals and that such consumption can occur without deleterious effects. Even if one believes this, as we have already seen in previous chapters, one might still decide to become a vegetarian, a pescetarian or a vegan.

One might consider it natural for humans to eat non-human animals, and one might even idolise the hunter-gatherer lifestyle of our ancestors and the remaining tribes which still have this lifestyle. However, one might be dismayed by the way 'food' animals are treated in industrialised societies – typically as resources where the priority is not well-being but profit maximisation.

So, one might believe that it is this contempo-rary treatment of animals that leads to unacceptable suffering and/or deleterious health effects in the humans who eat meat and/or increased violence in human society. Whereas, one might believe that if animals are viewed as individuals and treated with respect that eating them does not lead to such deleterious outcomes.

As we have seen, if one has such a view as this, then there is a good chance that one might decide to become a pescetarian rather than a vegetarian or a vegan (possibly due to believing that both human health worries, and concerns over increased violence, are less in fish consumption than non-fish meat consumption). However, it is also likely that one will not be so happy about the creation and growth of 'fish farms'.

Alternatively, one might be able to buy meat from sources where one knows that the animals have a relatively 'happy'/'natural' existence and are treated and killed in a humane manner, rather than buying and eating factory farmed meat.

I believe that a lot of vegetarians (a majority?) fall into the category which I am outlining in this chapter. That is to say, a lot of vegetarians believe that if the circumstances are right then it is acceptable for humans to eat animals. The question is: In which circumstances is such consumption acceptable? The answer will vary depending on the individual. However let us consider two scenarios.

Firstly, many vegetarians (and vegans) seem to believe that it is 'natural' and acceptable for Eskimos who live in the vicinity of the Arctic Circle to ice-fish and to consume the fish which they manage to catch. This implies that they believe that there is nothing *in principle* wrong with humans eating non-human animals.

Secondly, many vegetarians (and vegans) would surely accept that it is acceptable for a human to eat a non-human animal if the very survival of the human depended on such an act of eating. There are many possible scenarios in which this could apply, and the Eskimos are possibly one example. Another example would be when a human, or a group of humans, are stranded in a place without alternative food sources.

These scenarios seem to indicate that a lot of vegetarians don't have a problem with the basic principle of a human eating a non-human animal. Rather, they perhaps believe that the world would be a better place for all if such acts of eating were minimised and only occurred in special situations;

and perhaps they believe that when such acts of eating do occur that the eaten animal should be treated with respect. I am suggesting that the majority of vegetarians might actually have this opinion. That is to say, they believe that there is nothing in principle wrong with a human eating a non-human animal, but that the world that we currently live in, and the attitudes that we currently have as a society towards non-human animals, conspire to make large-scale consumption of animals undesirable. The world could be a better place without such consumption; the world would perhaps be more peaceful and people healthier.

Chapter 5

Conclusions

I have considered four different groups of reasons why people might decide to become a vegetarian, a pescetarian or a vegan. Some people simply believe that it is wrong for a human to eat a non-human animal because all animals are intrinsically valuable. There are possibly some people who have such a strong conviction in this belief that if their life depended on eating a non-human animal they would rather die than so eat. I have suggested that only a small minority of people actually fall into this group; most people surely believing that in certain circumstance the eating of a non-human animal by a human is acceptable. And most people also surely believe that there is a division between animals – it being acceptable to eat some animals and not acceptable to eat other animals.

The second group of beliefs I have outlined is centred on the idea that eating animals is bad for the health of the eater. We have seen that this could be because one believes that the human digestive system/body is not fully compatible with such consumption, that one believes that the food production systems that are prevalent are themselves not 'healthy', or that because one believes that suffering on the part of the animal becomes embedded into the body of the eater. So, whatever view one takes on the intrinsic value of animals, one can still believe that it is sensible for one to be a vegetarian, a vegan or a pescetarian.

The third group of beliefs is centred on the idea that treating animals as food sources creates a 'violent attitude' which ultimately leads to a plethora of undesirable knock-on effects. One such effect is an increased likelihood of the killer of animals being violent to other humans. Another such effect is the increased likelihood of humans who are not directly involved with acts of violence towards animals being more likely to be more violent towards other humans.

Living in a society with a high level of violence seems to be less conducive for one's personal health and well-being than living in a society with a low level of violence. So, there are obvious links between the belief in the link between animal killing/violence and increasing violence in human society, *and* the belief that eating animals is directly bad for one's health. In other words, one could believe that these two factors are mutually reinforcing and that they jointly conspire to make vegetarianism, veganism or pescetarianism desirable.

Again, whatever view one takes on the intrinsic value of some, or all, animals, and whatever view one takes on the direct health impacts of eating meat, one might have here a good reason to be a vegetarian, a vegan or a pescetarian.

Should I be a Vegetarian?

The fourth group of beliefs I have outlined is centred on the belief that eating animals is in principle acceptable and is an activity which can be largely free of deleterious effects; the problem is that the way that animals are currently typically treated causes a number of serious concerns which can cause one to become a vegetarian, a vegan or a pescetarian. Such concerns are a concern for the animals themselves, the belief that the ill treatment of animals can directly result in the ill health of humans, and the belief that such treatment can indirectly lead to increases in violence between humans. According to this view, if we could learn to view animals as individuals and treat them with respect then eating them would not result in such deleterious effects.

There are many links between the four groups of beliefs that I have outlined, and there are many different subtle positions within these various groups. This makes for a complex interconnecting web of beliefs, some of which will be mutually supporting, and some of which will be contradictory. For example, there are a multitude of different views on the question of whether there is a significant division between non-human animals, and if such a division exists where exactly it exists. Where one draws such a distinction could determine whether one becomes a pescetarian or a vegetarian. Furthermore, one can take a plethora of different views on the various animal products – such as milk, eggs and honey. One can also take a variety of views as to whether or not the use of animal products have the same level of deleterious impacts as the use of animals for meat. One can also change one's beliefs according to the situation – one can believe that fish are intrinsically valuable and shouldn't be eaten by humans, and also that this same consumption becomes acceptable if the life of a human depends on it. Why? Because one can believe that a human contains more intrinsic value than a fish, but that if it is possible for humans to exist without eating fish then the world would be a more healthy and peaceful place to live.

So, there is a web of intermingling factors at play – some reinforcing, some contradictory; each individual human will have their own individual web. It is this web as a whole which will determine the decision that an individual takes as to whether or not to become a vegetarian, a vegan or a pescetarian.

What about me – the pescetarian that I currently am? I am happy to be free of the factory farming of non-fish animals and aim to stay this way in the future. I believe this to be beneficial for my health and to have a range of other positive benefits (I am inclined to believe in the possibility of all of the potentially deleterious effects of eating meat outlined in both *Chapter Two* and *Chapter Three*). I shall also aim to continue to reduce my intake of dairy products for the same reasons. I am still feeling that it is right for me to eat fish, but I should be careful and try to check out where the fish has come from. I might also try to eat slightly less fish. The next time that someone asks me why I am a pescetarian I shall be prepared with a fairly long answer!

Hopefully this book might help you to make some decisions concerning your future diet too.